18 Stones

To Jeannie and Susan with love.

N.P. *and* S.L.R.

Our thanks to:

Chaja Verveer

Anita Kassof, ASSOCIATE DIRECTOR,
The Jewish Museum of Maryland

Paula Bogert, GRAPHIC DESIGNER

Gail G. Green, PROJECT PHOTOGRAPHER

And Karen Falk, JoAnn Fruchtman, Beth Grafman,
Patrick Harrington, Barry Narlines, Jesse Roth.

N.P. *and* S.L.R.

Made possible by an anonymous donation.
With additional support from the
Morris Schapiro and Family Foundation,
Barbara and Jay Katz.

The Jewish Museum of Maryland is an agency of
THE ASSOCIATED: Jewish Community Federation of Baltimore.

ISBN: 978-1-883312-11-4

18 Stones

NANCY PATZ · SUSAN L. ROTH

THE
Jewish Museum
OF MARYLAND
AT THE HERBERT BEARMAN CAMPUS

FOREWORD

We have chosen 18 photographs of people who lived in
The Netherlands before World War II. These became the
inspiration for 18 prose poems and 18 drawings, our tribute to
those whose lives were severely changed or stopped short by that
war. Traces of those lives are thin and pale or not there at all.

We were privileged to have had access to photographs from
the Verveer Collection of Holocaust Museum Houston.
As we studied the faded gray or sepia images, we came to
know the people in the photographs. In clear voices they
told us about themselves.

With words and drawings we began to interpret the images,
telling stories that became almost real to us. Fiction can be a
way to compensate for missing memory. Specific memories,
real or imagined, can describe a relationship, a gentle mood,
happy times—normal times—before the war.

In Jewish tradition people place small stones, symbolic tributes,
on the gravestones of people they wish to honor, respect,
remember. And so we offer our 18 symbolic stones—to imagine,
and to honor, respect, and remember this family and all
families whose histories were lost in the Holocaust.

Nancy Patz
Susan L. Roth
Baltimore, Maryland
January 2011

TABLE OF CONTENTS

Boy on Bridge

How old were you then?
About twelve, I would say.
I remember that suit.
It was new, big on me.
My mother told me
I looked like a man.
You look so old-fashioned.
What do you want?
It was sixty years ago!
How come your pants
are all bunched up?
I wore bicycle clips—
they kept the trousers
away from the wheels
while I rode.
They look pretty weird.
I suppose they do, but they worked.
Where were you standing?
Near our house, on a bridge.
With water underneath?
Yes, way down below.
Your hair was so black.
It was, it was bushy and black.
Why is your hand in your pocket?
You think I can remember that?
It was sixty years ago, my love.
Look how you're smiling.
But I wasn't at first.
"Stand straight, face the sun,
smile, dear," my mother said.
"*Smile*, dear," my father said.
"Wait, Mozes," my mother said.
 (They called me Mozes then.)
"Smile, dear, a *big* smile.
Say herring!" my mother said.
"Herring!" I said,
 and I started to laugh.
"Done!" said my father.

Grandpa, when you were standing there
laughing on that sunny day,
did you ever, ever think
I'd see your picture?
Never!
Not even once?
If I had known about you then, my love,
I would have had a smile,
without the herring,
reaching from here to Amsterdam.

Hendrik, the Piano Player

Hendrik wasn't only in jewelry you know,
even though I can tell you
he was a very good jeweler,
very successful. He made plenty of money.
But he could play the piano
like nobody's business.
I should know. I was there when he started.
The day he had his first lesson?
I remember it like yesterday.

My Mama taught him.
She taught everyone those days.
Hendrik, he was a great talent,
and he was smart.
People think it's all talent.
Hah! And you have to work hard, too,
if you're any good.
And Hendrik? Soon he was playing
better than I was. Even though Mama
had started teaching me
practically the day I was born.

We would sometimes play together—
duets, at Mama's little recitals.
Already then I thought he was handsome.
He never noticed me like THAT,
but we were friends.
At that age it was enough.

But time passed and sometimes, you know,
while we were playing together
our fingers would touch, or our shoulders
or our knees. I liked that, I admit it.
But Hendrik,
always so serious, working so hard
on his piano or his schoolwork,
he never said a word.
Maybe he was too shy, I don't know.

So.
After awhile I thought, enough of this nonsense.
I was seventeen already.
When our fingers touched
it felt like little electric shocks to me.

One day Hendrik and I were playing,
a four-hands Beethoven.
On purpose, I crossed way over.
I picked up his hands off the keys.
"What?" he said,
like a little absent-minded professor.
"Hendrik," I said. "Hendrik, do you love me?"
Hendrik, he woke up then.
He didn't let go of my hands.
"Yes," he said, very serious.
"I love you!" he said. *"I love you!"*
It was like he just realized it.
Then he laughed and put his arms around me.
We kissed each other,
and that was that.
It was forever,
and we both knew it, right then.

So we finished school,
we became engaged,
we were married,
he went into his father's business,
I helped out in the store,
and then we had Jacob,
then Amalia and Mathilde, the twins,
and then Rachel, the baby.
Mama taught them all to play the piano.
They were good, too,
but none of them could ever play
like Hendrik.

The Recipe for Apple Cake

"Well, I certainly do like a good piece of apple cake,
  who doesn't? I'd love another piece, Grete."
"Your apple cake is still the best.
  What I want to know is
  how two people can follow
  the exact same recipe
  and still it never tastes the same."

"Now, now,
  you know the recipe as well as I, Celine.
  Six eggs,
  two hundred grams of butter,
  three hundred grams of flour
  a little cream to moisten,
  two hundred grams of sugar
  measured to the top,
  two healthy dashes of vanilla,
  a pinch of nutmeg,
  a layer of marzipan right out of the can.
  We don't have to grind the almonds like our mothers did.
  The cinnamon.
  The cream of tartar—
  who knows what it does, but don't dare leave it out.
  That's all."
"Maybe it's the cutting of the apples!"
"Don't be silly. What's the difference
  if you keep the pips out?
  But this fresh cream is good,
  sliding over the edges,
  whipped not too stiff,
  with a sprinkling of confectioner's sugar."

"Grete, I'm tasting lemon!"
"Yes, the zest, of course.
  It adds a little something, yes?"
"That's not fair!
  Lemons aren't in the recipe!"
"So what. Everyone knows you have to have lemons."
"Grete, you should have told me about the lemons!"
"Oh, come on. Another piece, Celine? Just a sliver?"
"No! Well, just a sliver."

The Girl in the Big New Hat

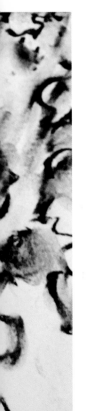

Sweetheart,
memory is an amazing thing.
Are you still too young to know this?
Listen,
here I am, your old grandmother,
about to make lunch
for my young lady granddaughter,
in my own house,
in my own country,
the United States of America.

But when I look at myself in this picture,
I'm that young lady again,
right now,
at home in The Hague.
In those days
America was a foreign land,
some big place, too big,
and far across the ocean
where they spoke a language
I could not understand.
It was a place full of cowboys
and gangsters
and buildings tall as mountains;
a place I had no friend;
a place I supposed
I would never go.

In those days
I had only wanted to go to Paris
to practice my schoolgirl *merci beaucoups*,
to eat croissants,
to walk along the Seine,
to spend all day at the Louvre whenever it rained.
In those days
I had never even dreamed a dream
about America.

I was just a young lady myself, you know?
I was a girl,
with a big new hat,
standing in the warm sun
on the way to *my* grandmother's house
for lunch.

The Marriage of Grietje and Aron

Aron,
do you take this woman?
To be your lawful wedded wife?
To love and to cherish?
This woman?
You mean my own true love?
Whom I love more than life itself?
My beautiful love?
The one I watched since she was sixteen?
And waited and waited for, till now?
My Grietje? Who secretly confessed to me
that she had done the same for me?
The one I am destined to marry
by the very grace of God?
The one for whom I have a love as pure
as the light of all mornings?
And a love as deep as from here to China?
With whom my heart is as full
as a cup running over?
The one who is mine
as I am hers?

Yes.

And it will be so
till the end of all time
forever and forever.

Grietje,
do you take this man?
To be your lawful wedded husband?
To love and to cherish?

This man?
My Aron?
Some are born to be together.
Some are destined, put upon this earth
to find each other
and they must be lucky in their searches.
It doesn't always happen.
But when it does,
each one knows from the very first instant.
It's then that life begins.
It's then that joy begins.
And it grows and it grows
and deepens
through all of time
and it never ends.
And for my Aron and me,
this is how it is.
Do I take this man?
I thank God.

Yes.

Grietje and Aron,
married, 1936.
The Hague, The Netherlands.

Little Man

Look at that!
Right on time!
How are you, little man?
I have a nice sheepskin just for you.
Tell your Mama not to worry, little man,
you won't fall off.
You know how many babies I've photographed?
I've been doing this
since before your Mama was born!
Maybe I even took *her* picture.
And not so long ago, either,
she looks so young,
(yes, you do, too, ma'am.)
Don't worry,
babies like the lights.

All right, little man,
are you ready to watch the birdie?
Give us a smile, little man,
come on, come on.
Good enough!
Look up now, little man.
There you are!
Big smile now.
What are you so worried about?
Your Mama's right here, see?
What are you going to be
when you get big?
Doctor? Lawyer?
Professor?
So handsome, this one.
So alert.

Look how he's following my every move.
Maybe you'll be a photographer, eh?
I could use a helper!
Right, little man?
Right?
Don't worry.
We're almost done.
Give me a smile, little man!
No? Never mind, never mind.
There we are, Ma'am.
We're all done.
You'll have a fine present
for the grandparents,
the aunts and uncles, too.
I'll make as many as you want.
Take your time, let me know.
They'll be ready in a week.

Next?
Look at that!
Right on time!
How are you, little man?
I have a nice sheepskin just for you.
Nothing to worry about …

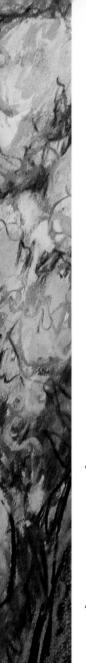

There Were So Many Pictures

All because of the party for Uncle Jonas,
Aunt Bertha invited everyone to the picnic.
First was the feast,
and then the cake,
almost big as the table.
Uncle Jonas blew out
fifty candles and another to grow on,
and after the cake
came the presents—
the books, the cufflinks,
the letter-openers, the paper weights,
and after all those
came the new camera.
Uncle Jonas read the card out loud.
"To Jonas
from your loving wife."
He hugged Aunt Bertha.
He twirled her around
as if they were dancing.
Then, in a very loud voice,
he announced to us all:
"This wonderful birthday
will go down in history.
And I shall make it happen.
Today I am going to take
everybody's picture!"

He turned to Aunt Bertha.
"You, my dear, shall be first," he said.
"Me?" said Aunt Bertha, "Oh, no, not me!"
She covered her face.
"Take pictures of the children," she said.
She peeked through her fingers,
then pointed to Clara and me,
sitting on a little wooden bench.
"Take a picture of the girls."
"Oh, come, Aunt Bertha,"
said our cousin Noach.
He led her by the hand.
"Stand here, with us!"
Aunt Bertha straightened her dress.
She tugged on her hat.
She patted her hair.
She licked her lips.
She pinched her cheeks.
"I look too old," she said.
"Nonsense, Auntie," Noach said.
He squeezed her shoulder,
gave her a kiss.
"You don't look *one day*
over a hundred and two!"
Aunt Bertha smiled.
She held her breath.
"One, two, *three!*" said Uncle Jonas,
and then he took the picture.

The Intellectual

Who? The one in the circle?
Oh, it's Cousin Aaron.
He was always dressed like that,
white shirt,
bow tie,
vest,
tweeds.
He wore his professorial clothes
like his skin.
I'm not sure he took them off
to take his bath
or go to bed.

Cousin Aaron was serious.
No nonsense,
no frivolities,
no hobbies, no vacations.
He hated picnics in the country.
He was shy,
he hid behind his books.
He stayed quiet,
though nice enough.
If you spoke with him,
you'd have to listen well
since everything he said
was thoughtful
and referenced with big, important books
that mostly only *he* had ever read.
In return you would receive
a rigorous, intellectual gift
of a new way of understanding.
No one else could think like Cousin Aaron.

Only once, at a family celebration,
indoors, of course,
Aaron became almost garrulous,
that is, for him.
Maybe he'd had an extra sip of wine.
He confessed
to feeling happiest
when he sat,
inside his heavy-curtained study,
late at night,
in the dark,
uninterrupted,
as he surveyed
the vast reaches of his own inner mind.
"Just like the Italian poet, Leopardi,"
said Cousin Aaron.
"You haven't read him? Oh,
for goodness sake,
you must."

That was Cousin Aaron.
White shirt,
bow tie,
vest,
tweeds,
head.

A Few Words Spoken at Effie's Funeral

I always called Effie "my wife's mother"
because, as I told her,
she was just too nice
to be "mother-in-law."
There are jokes about
awful mothers-in-law,
but honestly,
I can say nothing negative about Effie
except that she left us too soon.
Even after 93 years it was too soon.
Maybe you think I'm exaggerating
for this occasion.
I'm not.
This picture of us,
someone took it
on a golden afternoon.
My God, she looks so alive here …

I want to tell you a story
about the first time I met Effie.
Esther and I were keeping company.
Of course I had to meet her mother.
"You'll like her," Esther kept telling me.
But I was scared.
I was invited for lunch.
When I rang the bell,
Effie answered the door herself.
I watched her smile,
and before she even spoke
I knew I'd love her.
"David," she said, "I'm so happy.
Come in, come in."
She gave me her left hand.
Her right was covering her apron pocket,
and she didn't move it.

"Guess what I've got in my pocket!" she said.
I saw the pocket move.
"Come here, you infinitessimal thing," she said.
"Say hello to David."
Effie pulled out a tiny puff of black fur,
the smallest dog I have ever seen.
It trembled in her hand.
I saw dark, shining eyes
and a little pink tongue.
It whispered a bark.
"He's too young to leave his mother,
but I found him on the street.
What could I do?
Now he has a house
right in my pocket!" Effie laughed.
"And a mother, too!
Do you want to hold him?"
The tiny dog squirmed
in the palm of my hand.
He licked my finger.
"Well," said Effie, "there you are.
He likes you."

She put her hand on my arm.
She looked right into my eyes.
"That's good," she said, "because I do, too."

It was the beginning of a forty-year friendship,
not nearly long enough.

Max and Me

Just Max and me,
in front of the house,
Max in his hat.
Just Max and me,
taking a walk,
down the street
in front of the house.
Just Max and me,
out for a stroll,
a walk down the street
in front of the house.
"Get a breath of air,
get out of the house."
Just Max and me,
Max in his hat.
"Let's go outside,
it's plenty light,
we'll get some air."
Just me,
and Max in his hat.
We finished our tea,
we'll take a walk,
just Max and me.
"Just step outside,
it's nice outside,
you won't need a coat,
come, leave the dishes,
who's going to see?

Just step outside,
outside with me."
Just Max and me,
we'll take a walk,
in front of the house.
We finished our tea,
just Max and me.
"Come out for a while,
the sun is still high,
the weather is fine,
in front of the house
we'll walk a bit."
In front of the house,
just Max in his hat
and me.

Tea at Old Aunt Rosa's

Old Aunt Rosa
kept the curtains closed
even when the sun was shining
on those long, visiting afternoons.
Mama and Papa walked the three flights.
Jansje and I ran,
Jansje always faster.
At the door
I stood on my toes
to reach the brass lion knocker.
I banged as hard as I could.
Jansje always whispered, "Do it again!"
and I did.

Old Aunt Rosa, still holding her book,
opened the door.
She hugged us. The book between us
helped to keep her distance.
Her white-powder cheek smelled of old roses.
"Remember," she said.
"Do *not* touch the big doll."

We sat at her little square table
covered with tea-stained lace.
Old Aunt Rosa
poured our tea into flowery cups.
She squeezed the lemon.
She added sugars,
"one or two?"
She never spilled a grain.
Then came honey cake,
dry and bitter.
She used silver tongs
to pinch each piece.
We stabbed our slices
with her silver forks.

Once,
when old Aunt Rosa went
into the other room to get a book,
Jansje jumped up.
With both hands.

She lifted the big doll from its shelf
and turned her upside down.
She found at least a dozen petticoats, all lace,
and in the center, thin, white china legs
wearing long white bloomers
with ruffled edges.
Shiny black shoes were painted on her feet, and—
"Put that *back*!" Mama whispered.
"I mean it! Right *now*! Hurry *up*!"
Jansje hurried.
She turned the doll over,
shook her in her skirts,
put her back on the shelf,
sat her own self back down
at the lace-covered table,
her napkin in her lap,
and she even stabbed a second piece of honey cake,
although she never ate it,
all before old Aunt Rosa returned.
Mama sucked in her breath.
She gave Jansje such a look.
"Nietzsche says it better," said old Aunt Rosa,
as she handed the small leather-bound book to Papa.
"Ah, yes," he said. He turned a few pages.
I think I saw a little smile around his eyes,
but I'm not sure.

Ten minutes later we were allowed to leave.
Still smelling old roses
we ran from the door,
down the stairs,
jumping three steps at the bottom of each landing.
"Girls," Papa's voice chased after us,
"no running!"
But we were at the bottom,
out the door,
on the sidewalk,
hugging,
laughing till we snorted,
laughing, laughing.

"To Us!"

"To us!" Izak said,
  and he lifted his cup.
  Listen to him, I heard myself think.
  Listen to him. Could this be real?
  Was this happening?
  Did I love Izak?
  I mean, I did, of course, love Izak,
  but was it true-love-forever love?
  Did he love me?
  What was love?

  I did love him.
  We were best friends,
  we went everywhere together,
  we even studied together,
  we went to family parties together,
  and the relatives, the friends,
  they all were sure
  we would be together forever.
  But *love*?
  What did it mean?
  I didn't know.
  I was a young girl. I was scared.
  How would it be if we were … married?
  How could I leave Mama and Papa
  and Elisabeth and Isadore?
  How could I leave the house
  where I'd lived my whole life?
  Would I be the one to make the cocoa
  just like Mama?
  The one to do the shopping?
  to cook the suppers?
  to arrange the furniture?
  to watch over the maid?
  to lock the door at night?
  I, no longer young miss, but *Mrs.* instead?

  Izak lifted his cup again.
"Sara, your head is so far away.
  Come. Clink your glass to my cup,
  and you say it, too, *To us!*"

"Izak," I whispered, that was all.
"Sara, you're frightened!
  I feel it.
  Should we wait?
  Do you need time to think?
  I can wait, watch!"
  That was Izak,
  my best friend.
  He leaned back in his chair.
  He closed his eyes.
  He tapped his fingers on the table.
  He started to hum.

  What happened then?
  Well, Izak, he made funny faces
  that made me laugh,
  and then he was laughing, too,
  and once we were laughing
  I wasn't so worried,
  and so we married,
  and just like Mama
  I made the cocoa,
  did the shopping,
  cooked the suppers,
  arranged the furniture,
  watched over the maid,
  and locked the door at night,
  and …

Birds, Bees, Babies

Papa came out of the bedroom,
  smiling and smiling.
"You have a baby sister, darling!"
  He lifted me in a hug,
  he kissed both cheeks.
"A perfect little sister!
  You'll see her soon," he said,
"Where's Mama?" I asked.
"Resting," he said.
"Mama's tired now, you know."
"Where did the baby come from?" I asked.
"I didn't see anyone carry in a baby."
"Oh, my dear," said Aunt Judith, Mama's sister,
  who was sitting in the corner.
"I'll bet you didn't tell her *anything*!"
  She sniffed.
  But Papa was gone,
  back inside the bedroom.
"Where did Mama find the baby?"
  I asked a second time.
  Aunt Judith sat up straighter.
"I'll tell you everything, dear," she said.
"It's high time you knew."

I moved over, to stand in front of where she sat.
"You see, my dear," she began,
"it's all about the birdies and the bees, dear.
  Babies grow, birdies grow,
  and even little bees have babies, dear.
  It's the way of the world, dear.
  Even doggies have baby doggies, even
  pussycats have baby pussycats. Even little mice,
  and fish and even snakes and butterflies.
  And Mama, too, had your baby sister, dear.
  And well, my dear," Aunt Judith took a breath.
"It's like a tiny seed was planted.
  Yes, that's it! And then it grew and grew
  and like a little birdie or bumble bee,
  it waited, till today when it was time,
  and the baby wanted to meet you.
  And now you have a baby sister.
  Isn't that just grand, dear?
  And, dear," Aunt Judith looked away.
"There are some things
  a little girl cannot understand.
  You'll have to wait
  until you're older for the rest.
  But now, at least, you understand
  the most important parts,
  thanks to *me*, and not my sister
  or my brother-in-law.
  Now you know. Can you remember?"

Aunt Judith might have chirped forever
  if the door hadn't opened again.
  Papa came out.
"I've explained the ways of the world,"
  Aunt Judith reported, "and I'm pleased as punch.
  It's high time our Johanna understands what's what."

Early One Morning
on the Canal Boat with Papa

"Hurry!" Papa whispered,
 and I did,
 even though it was so cold
 and still dark
 that early Spring morning.
"Hurry, the canal boat will leave!"
 We rushed
 into the chilly, greyish light.
 Mama made me wear my coat,
 and I was glad.
 You can always take it off
 is what she said.

We were the first ones on the canal boat.
 There *had* been time
 for cocoa before we left,
 even though Papa said there wasn't,
 but never mind,
 because right after
 I chose my outdoor seat
 and Papa took my picture,
 we went inside
 where it was warm
 at the coffee bar.
 Papa brought a pot of hot cocoa
 to our little table,
 and lovely thick slices of bread,
 sweet buttered, covered
 with chocolate sprinkles.
 The boat began to move.

Back outside,
 the cool air felt good
 on our rosy cheeks.
 On the silver water,
 wavy, upside-down
 houses and bridges
 turned pale yellow,
 light blue,
 then brighter.
 When the chill was gone
 I took off my scarf
 and leaned back in my seat
 for the rest of the ride.

A Poem for Two Voices
Repeatedly Interrupting Each Other

What a good child, so pretty, so sweet.
Louis, have you ever seen such a beauty?
She's adorable, what can I say?
Tttt, tttt, tttt, such a love of a child.
Look at her, Hanna, look at those curls.
I want to pinch those rosy cheeks.
How did she get so pretty?
She's clever, too, Louis.
So smart, you can see it all
in those big black eyes.
And she knows her numbers already!
She knows her alphabet, too!
Imagine, Hanna, she's so young.
A little genius, I really mean it.
I can tell she's going to be musical.
Louis, would you look at those curls?
Hello, Beautiful.
Hello, Princess.
Hello, Honey.
What a beauty she is, such a love of a child.
We have a present for you, Hendrika.
A little sundress.
See the daisies?
Guess who embroidered them, every stitch,
just for Hendrika.
What a good child she is.
So quiet, so pretty, so sweet.
She's gorgeous.
Come here, Hendrika.

Meijer at 70, Josef at 72

Meijer? It's me.
Listen, you won't believe
what I found in a box of papers.
In the attic.
Listen.
I found this tiny picture
from God knows when
but I can make out Mother.
She's wearing some flowery dress.
And she's holding you, her little Meijer.
I'm right there with you.
The picture's small,
it's a miracle it didn't disappear
with all the rest.
We're in front of the old house,
you know, the one you think you remember
only because they told you about it so often.
Anyway, it's not a big deal,
but it was such a surprise
to find it tucked under the flap
on the bottom of the carton,
and I don't remember ever having seen it.
I'll copy it, sure, and stick it in an envelope.
No, I'll keep it on my desk—
aren't we seeing you on Friday?

Meijer at 70, Josef at 72

Dashing Uncle Emanuel

Dashing.
That was Uncle Emanuel:
tall, handsome,
charming, worldly, wealthy,
very smart.
My sister and I believed
he'd been everywhere there was to go,
seen everything there was to see;
we believed he knew all there was to know.
It was better than a birthday
when he came to visit.

Once, when I was older
and Uncle E. had just returned
from a faraway, exotic place,
he said he needed a little
civilization right away,
to sooth his wandering soul.
He invited my sister and me
to accompany him into town,
that very afternoon,
for a feast for the eyes, he said,
a surprise.
He wouldn't say what.

Arm in arm in arm
we walked,
across the little bridge,
down the street,
and on to the art museum,
a place we often went.
But Uncle Emanuel passed familiar galleries
and led us up back stairs
to offices we'd never seen.
He rang a bell.
We were invited in.
Our coats were taken.
We were asked to sit
at a wide oak table.
Green glass lamps were lit.
We waited.

A man came in,
pushing with effort a trolley of boxes.
His white-cotton-gloved hands
held such gloves for each of us.
Then, with our white-cotton-gloved hands folded,
we waited again,
watching the man place the first box on the table.
He lifted the top,
lifted a white linen cover.
Uncle Emanuel took a matted picture from the box,
placed it on the table between us,
opened the mat on its hinges,
slipped away a waxy-looking paper
to show us a sepia drawing.

"Rembrandt could draw," said Uncle Emanuel.
He sighed.
"Would you look at that scratchy brown line?"

We spent all afternoon looking
at Rembrandt's sepia lines,
drawing after drawing
from box after box of treasure.

At dusk a bell rang.
The trolley man returned
to wheel the boxes away.

Outside,
in sepia light,
the sky, the streets, the buildings,
even the cobblestones,
were scribbled and scratched
in Rembrandt's own hand.
An old man wearing a tattered brown coat
stood in the lamp light
with a wash of brown shadow behind him.
Arm in arm in arm again
Rembrandt drew us
through the sepia evening
towards home.

Letter to Rebecca

13 October 1941

My dear Rebecca,

You sounded so worried in your letter. Please, don't be. We're fine. Don't believe all you read in your papers. I enclose a photo. See how the boys have grown? Don't they look happy, carried by their Papa? Don't they look healthy? Believe me. We're all fine, Anna, too. There are political rumblings, yes, but there are always rumblings, you know that.

I think the manuscript will be finished in a few weeks. And, can you imagine? I think I've already decided on the topic for my next book … but I'm not going to tell you about it until this one is really finished.

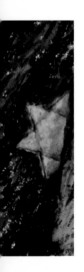

Anna is editing for me. Lately we've been working together every evening, after the boys go to bed, in the little study off the dining room. Do you remember it? It's so comfortable there, just the two of us—me at my writing desk, and Anna, on the chaise, wrapped in her paisley shawl, looking beautiful as always, reading, with her red pencil in her hand. If the prose reads well, it will be because of her, not me. We sit, drinking tea, working quietly, only occasionally speaking. It's a special time of the day for us.

The boys are all in school now, the twins are in the second class, already reading, can you believe it? Boas is in the first. He knows his alphabet and numbers. I love to watch them playing together, running, pushing, shoving, like little bear cubs, nothing malicious. And it's funny to hear the twins explaining the ways of the world to Boas. They're protective of their brother. Very sweet. Mama and Papa are fine, too. We go to them on Sundays, like always, with the others. Mama still cooks the big lunch for everyone and won't accept any help.

But we all miss you and Elias, and the children. It's hard to imagine them so grown up, thinking about university already! Maybe one day, when the book is finished, we could all … oh, I don't know. The ocean is so wide, America so far, the passage so expensive. Still, how we would love to see you all!

But we shall talk again about a visit, as soon as the book is done. Meanwhile, please, you must stop the worrying. Life goes on, almost like before, and we are happy.

Our love to all of you,

Simon

I. Two Stories of Survival

Chaja Verveer does not remember most of her family in the photographs that inspired *18 Stones*. The snapshots were taken in Holland in the late 1930s, just before the country fell to Nazi Germany, and in the early months of World War II. Chaja was born in September, 1941, as the anti-Semitism of the Nazi puppet government in Amsterdam was intensifying. The following summer the Nazis began deporting Dutch Jews to the death camps.

That Chaja survived is extraordinary. In the autumn of 1942, her family separated to go into hiding. Chaja, alone, was sent to live with a gentile family named van den Berg. But at the beginning of 1944, the van den Bergs were arrested. Chaja was sent without them to Westerbork, a transit camp in northeast Holland, then to Bergen Belsen, and finally to Theresienstadt, the ghetto concentration camp that served as a staging ground for deportations to the death camps. Despite terrible privations, Chaja was an appealing and attractive toddler, and strangers took care of the little girl. She was liberated from Theresienstadt in May, 1945. Chaja was not yet four years old.

After the war Chaja was reunited with her mother and her three brothers, who had survived in separate hiding places. Her father had been executed for his association with the Resistance, and most of her extended family perished in the Holocaust—as did more than 80 percent of the Dutch Jews, the highest percentage of any country in Europe.

The photographs' survival is also remarkable. When the family members went into hiding, they abandoned their home and all of their belongings. Later, authorities emptied the Verveers' house and placed their possessions in the attic of the local primary school, where the headmaster's son found them. Discovering a box of photos among the household goods, he gave them to Jet Ouwens, a gentile girl who had befriended the Verveers. Jet may not have realized that she was assuming a terrible risk: if she had been found with images of a Jewish family there might have been grave consequences.

After the war was over, Jet located Chaja's mother and returned the photographs to her. Decades later, after Mrs. Verveer's death, Jet renewed contact with Chaja and her brothers. Although they remained in touch, they never discussed the photographs. In the summer of 2010—sixty-five years after the war ended—Jet was reminded of the photographs when her old friend, the headmaster's son, visited her. It was only then that Jet told the Verveers that she, at age thirteen, had saved the visual record of their family's pre-war life.

II. In Their Own Voices

In 2007, artist Nancy Patz and author Susan L. Roth decided to collaborate
on a project about Jewish life in Holland before World War II. At Holocaust
Museum Houston Patz asked to see photographic collections that might
serve as visual references. She was introduced to Chaja Verveer, who had
loaned her family photographs to the Museum. Verveer sent Patz and
Roth copies of the photographs without any background information.

The lack of detail about the photos was fortuitous, because it freed Roth to
create new narratives. She conjured an imaginary constellation of individual
stories and family relationships that, in fact, bear no resemblance to the
Verveers' pre-war experiences.

The photographs inspired Patz to draw portraits infused with sensitivity and
vitality. They are, like Roth's prose poems, products of imagined memory.

When *18 Stones* was nearing completion, Patz invited Chaja Verveer to her
studio for a preview of the project. Patz and Roth were a bit apprehensive
before she arrived: What if the drawings were upsetting to her? What if she
were to resent the fiction of the prose poems? What if she were to hate the
whole project? But artist and writer need not have been concerned. Verveer
was and is an enthusiastic supporter. *18 Stones* represents all families
whose pasts have been lost.

They are remembered with respect and honor.

Perhaps this is why the photographs survived.

Anita Kassof
Associate Director
The Jewish Museum of Maryland
Baltimore, Maryland
January 2011